H

by Kim Fields

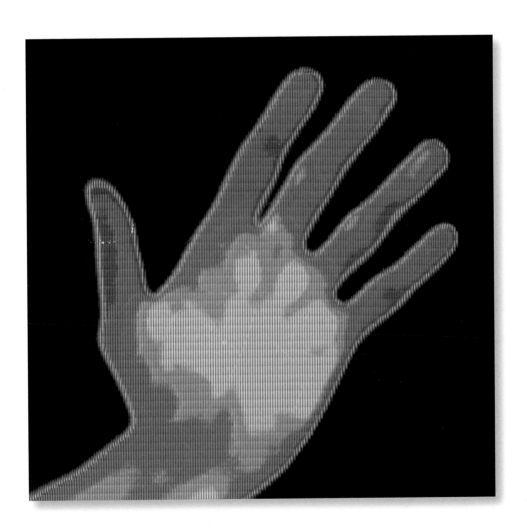

Why does matter have energy?

Energy in Matter

Energy is the ability to do work or cause a change. You use energy to make heat when you rub your hands together. Cool hands become warmer ones. All changes need energy. Energy is used when there is a change to how something looks, what it is made of, or where it is.

Tiny moving particles make up all matter. Particles are tightly packed in a solid. They only move slightly. In a liquid, particles are close together. They flow freely. Particles are far apart in a gas. They move all around. Particles move because they have energy.

Thermal energy is energy due to moving particles that make up matter. We feel the flow of thermal energy as heat. An object's particles move faster as it gets hotter. An object's particles move more slowly as it cools.

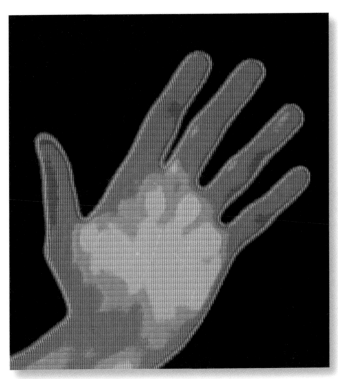

Colors in this heat picture show the different amounts of heat energy.

Measuring Moving Particles

Temperature is often measured with a thermometer. One type of thermometer is a glass tube with a bulb that holds colored alcohol. The degrees are shown by numbered lines on the outside of the glass tube. The lines on one side of the tube tell the degrees Fahrenheit. The lines on the other side tell the degrees Celsius.

Matter expands, or gets larger, when its particles move faster. It contracts, or gets smaller, when particles slow down. If a thermometer touches matter with fast-moving particles, the particles in the colored alcohol speed up. They also move farther apart. The liquid expands and moves up inside the tube. The number on the line shows a higher temperature. The liquid in the tube contracts if the particles slow down. The number on the line shows a lower temperature.

The thermometer has to be on or in what it's measuring. If the thermometer is not touching the substance, it might not measure the motion of the particles correctly.

Heat and Temperature

The particles of a material move fast when the material has a high temperature. But temperature is not a measure of how much heat a material has.

People often mix up the meanings of heat and temperature. Temperature is the measure of the average amount of particle motion in matter. It measures the average energy. Thermal energy measures the total energy of moving particles. It measures how fast particles move and how many are moving. Heat is the movement of thermal energy from one material to another.

Suppose you filled a large pot and a small pot halfway with boiling water. The large pot holds more water. It has many more moving water particles. This means it has more energy of motion. Because of this, the large pot has more thermal energy. The temperature of the water in both pots is the same because the water in each pot is boiling. The average amount of particle motion is also the same. The size of the pot does not change the temperature.

How does heat move?

Conduction

Thermal energy flows from a warmer material to a cooler one. The movement is what we feel as heat. A heat source gives off energy that can be taken in by particles of matter. Heat energy moves by conduction between two solids that are touching. **Conduction** happens when heat energy is transferred by one thing touching another.

The metal spoon conducts heat well. This causes the piece of wax on the spoon to melt. The wooden spoon does not conduct heat well. The piece of wax on this spoon does not melt.

Place one end of a cool metal spoon in boiling water. What happens? The spoon gets hot! Particles in the spoon touch the hot water. They start to move quickly. The particles crash into other particles in the spoon's handle. Soon heat energy moves throughout the spoon. The transfer of energy continues until the water and the spoon are the same temperature.

If you do the same thing with a wooden spoon, its handle will stay cool. That is because the wooden spoon does not conduct heat energy very well.

Conductors and Insulators

A **conductor** is a material that allows heat to move through it easily. Many metals, such as iron, aluminum, and copper, are good conductors. An iron pan gets hot quickly when it is placed on a heat source, such as a burner. A metal spoon is also a good conductor.

Iron pan

Some things do not get warm even when they touch something hot. An **insulator** is a material that doesn't let much heat pass through it. Wood is a very good insulator. That is why many pots have wooden handles.

Marble is an insulator. It has been used in buildings since ancient times. Plastic foam combines two good insulators: plastic and air. Plastic foam containers keep your food warm and your hands cool.

Plastic foam cup

Marble tray

Convection

A fluid is matter that does not have a definite shape. Liquids and gasses are fluids. Heated fluids can move from place to place in a process called convection.

A **convection current** is a pattern of flowing heat energy. A convection current forms when a heated fluid expands. Heat moves through air in a convection current. When air is heated, it becomes less dense than the cooler air around it. The cooler air sinks below the warmer air. This forces the warm air upward. The cycle continues as more cool air is warmed and is forced upward by colder air.

A radiator heats the air by convection.

What is the heat source in this photo? It's the candles. As long as the candles are burning, movement of the rising warm air will make the objects above the candles move. The energy from the flames heats the air above them. The air particles move faster and farther apart. This makes the air less dense. Cooler air rushes under the less dense air. It pushes the warm air upward.

Much larger convection currents change our weather. Uneven heating of the air around Earth causes large currents. They make Earth's major wind patterns.

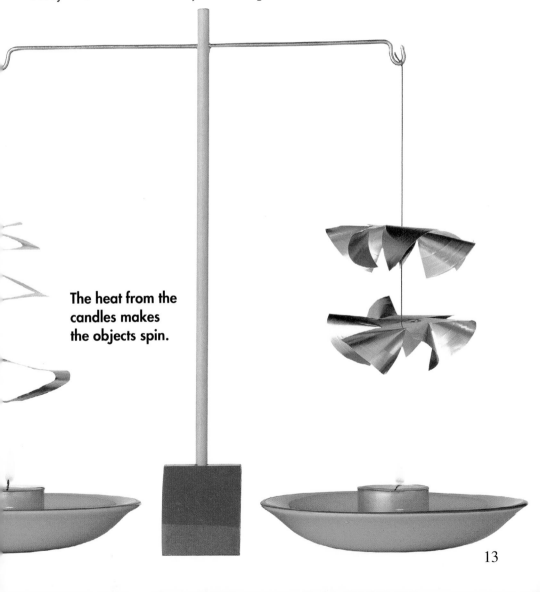

The heat from the candles makes the objects spin.

Radiation

Radiation is energy sent out in little bundles. You feel radiation when you get warm in the Sun or sit by a fire.

Radiation can travel through empty space or through matter. It is absorbed by dark, dull surfaces. Shiny surfaces reflect radiation. Clear surfaces allow radiation inside. A greenhouse is made of plastic or glass. Radiation from sunlight makes a greenhouse warm even when it is cold outside.

Radiation is unlike conduction and convection. Conduction happens when materials are touching each other. Convection needs the heated particles of a fluid to carry energy. Radiation does not need particles of solids, liquids, or gases. Radiation can move energy great distances, even from the Sun to Earth.

Conduction, Convection, and Radiation

Energy from the Sun heats Earth's surface through radiation. The surface transfers heat to the air and warms it through conduction. Convection currents also form as Earth's surface heats the air. These currents cause Earth's wind and rain patterns.

Energy is the ability to do work. Heat is the transfer of thermal energy. It can be moved in several ways. Conduction, convection, and radiation are all ways that heat is moved. Think about how heat moves the next time you drink hot cocoa, sit in a warm sunbeam, or take a hot bath.

Glossary

conduction
the transfer of heat energy by one thing touching another

conductor
a material that allows heat to move easily through it

convection current
a pattern of flowing heat energy

insulator
a material that limits the amount of heat that passes through it

radiation
energy sent out in little bundles

thermal energy
energy due to moving particles that make up matter